HERITAGE

HERITAGE

90 Years, from the Three Wheeler to the Cobra

SIMON TAYLOR
& PETER BURN

First published in Great Britain in 1996
by Osprey, an imprint of Reed Consumer Books Limited
Michelin House, 81 Fulham Road, London SW3 6RB
and Auckland, Melbourne, Singapore and Toronto

ISBN 1 85532 534 9

Managing Editor: Shaun Barrington
Edited by Judith Millidge
Design by Paul Kime

Printed in Hong Kong

FRONT COVER *For many AC enthusiasts, the definitive classic Cobra is
an unmodified, factory-correct Mk II. Colin Sanders has owned his
pristine example for 15 years*

BACK COVER *Tim Oldrey's 1936 16/70 tourer is the epitome of the
elegant pre-war sports car*

HALF TITLE PAGE *Around the base of the 1930s radiator mascot was the
legend: "Greyhound of the Road"*

TITLE PAGE *Two of David Hescroff's magnificent AC stable at home. In
the foreground is his 1936 four-seater tourer. Behind is "Monty", the
famous 1930 Ray Morley trials car with body from the Montlhéry
record-breaker: see page 24*

ABOUT THE AUTHOR AND PHOTOGRAPHER:

SIMON TAYLOR has spent his life writing and talking about motorcars.
At 23 he was editor of the motor-racing weekly *Autosport*, going on to
launch *What Car?* and *Classic and Sportscar* for its proprietors
Haymarket, and mastermind their acquisition of *Autocar*. Nowadays he
is Haymarket Magazine's Chairman, as well as BBC Radio's commen-
tator on Grand Prix racing. He lives in Chiswick, London, with one
wife, two children, four cats and eight cars.

PETER BURN has been a professional motorcar photographer for more
than 25 years. He was chief photographer in turn on *Autosport*, *Motor*,
and *Autocar*, before setting up his own freelance business in 1994. His
commissions include Osprey's *Jaguar XJ220* (author Philip Porter), the
definitive work, and take him to motor shows, races, and car launches
all over the world. In between, he lives with his family in
Wallington, Surrey, England.

ABOVE *The 1980s Mk IV Cobra recreated the spirit of the Mk III of two decades earlier, while complying with US legislation. These appropriately-registered cars, with 5-litre Mustang 302 V8s on Holley carburettors, both belong to AC Owners Club officers: Subs Secretary Barry Howsley and Exhibitions Co-ordinator Eric Gates*

CONTENTS

INTRODUCTION

THE STORY OF AC SPANS 90 years, almost the entire history of the motor car. It is one of crisis and success, of swings of fortune from boom to bust, of changes of ownership, of strong personalities – Weller and Portwine, Edge, the Hurlock family, Rudd and Shelby, Angliss.

And it is one of astonishing variety. What other car manufacturer's lineage ranges from delivery tricycles and invalid carriages to thundering monsters that beat Ferrari in a World Championship? Or from svelte, fashionable 1930s sports cars to an idiosyncratic fibreglass coupé with transverse engine and chain drive?

During the 1920s, when AC first became a serious manufacturer of quality cars, there were 380 car manufacturers in Britain alone. By 1995 precisely ten of those marques remained: only four were in British ownership, and just two were independent. AC was one of them.

Even though the long heritage of AC is so varied, a common thread runs through it. Every AC ever built is a car of character. All reward their owners with enter-tainment and stimulus at the wheel, and usually with elegance. Most people who succumb to their charms remain hooked, and forsake other types of car. Time and again one finds an owner who has sold his AC under the influence of another, briefer, infatuation – and has then not rested until he has been able to buy it back again.

AC owners vary like their cars, which can have such wildly differing values and performance. But, as membership of the AC Owners' Club will demonstrate, they are without exception a friendly, patient and enthusiastic lot. In putting this book together around the photographic talents of Peter Burn, who travelled far and wide to shoot camera-worthy ACs, I owe much thanks to the owners and club members who gave so much time and trouble to help in the search.

I must acknowledge my debt to the various ACOC section registrars, and also to that indefatigable AC historian John McLellan: his two books on AC, published in the early 1980s and long out of print, are still by far the best on the marque.

RIGHT *The joys of AC ownership: a sunny day, a country road, and an Ace on full song. Still worthy of the enthusiasm of road-tester John Bolster (actually praising the Ace-Bristol) forty years ago: 'This is it! At last Britain has produced a sports car with independent four-wheel suspension, which holds the road as well as any Continental car.'* (Autosport, May 18, 1956)

WELLER AND PORTWINE

THE STORY OF AC'S BIRTH has often been told. At the start of the century a clever young engineer, John Weller, was backed by John Portwine, a prosperous South London businessman with a string of butchers' shops, to enter the mushrooming motorcar business.

Their first effort, an ambitious 20 hp touring car, was exhibited at the 1903 Crystal Palace Motor Show under the Weller name. But it would have been too expensive to produce, and instead Portwine encouraged Weller to ponder the needs of his meat delivery boys, who relied on bicycles and horse-drawn vans to serve their customers.

He came up with a little wooden-framed three-wheeler truck, powered by a 636 cc single-cylinder air-cooled engine and steered with a tiller. The box for the meat was between the front wheels and the engine was under the driver's seat, driving the rear wheel by chain. He called it the Auto-Carrier, and by 1904 it was in production.

Quicker and more efficient than bicycles and horses, and at a cost of just £85, the Auto-Carrier caught on quickly. It was bought by newspaper publishers, bakers, laundries and grocers, as well as big retailers like Selfridges, Army & Navy Stores, Dickens & Jones and Boots. One company had a fleet of over 70. As the AC company history, published in the 1950s, points out, it predated by at least half a century the now familiar sight of the rep thrashing his company car:

> "They were mostly handled by youths of 17 years. In that age the spirit of adventure thrived on the roads and, as traffic bluebottles were less in evidence than they are today, the boys were inclined to race every other Auto-Carrier they met ..."

From this to a passenger version was an easy step. In 1907 the Auto-Carrier Sociable appeared, with a second seat in place of the goods box, and for the first time Auto-Carrier was abbreviated to AC, using the curved art-nouveau lettering that remains to this day. This was followed by a three-seater with room for two in front of the driver, and then the definitive version with driver and one passenger side by side at the front. There was a military variant, with two soldiers in front turned round to face the man at the tiller, and in one case an entrepreneurial entertainer built a travelling Punch & Judy show on an Auto-Carrier chassis.

A Sociable was timed at a dizzy 47 mph at Brooklands, and several were entered for the popular reliability trials of the day. For many, the Sociable was their first experience of motoring. Several intrepid owners toured Europe, and Sociables were exported as far afield as India, South Africa, Malaysia and Japan.

Riding on this success, the burgeoning little company moved in 1911 from its original South London works at West Norwood to an attractive setting by the river at Thames Ditton in Surrey. It was to remain there for three-quarters of a century.

A four-wheeler was bound to follow, and in 1913 Weller produced a sporty little two-seater with the gearbox in unit with the back axle. A French Fivet engine was used, but only a handful of cars were built before the outbreak of World War 1 – during which the Thames Ditton workshop (displaying for the first time the versatility that would repeatedly get them through difficult times ahead) made their contribution to the war effort by making shells and fuses.

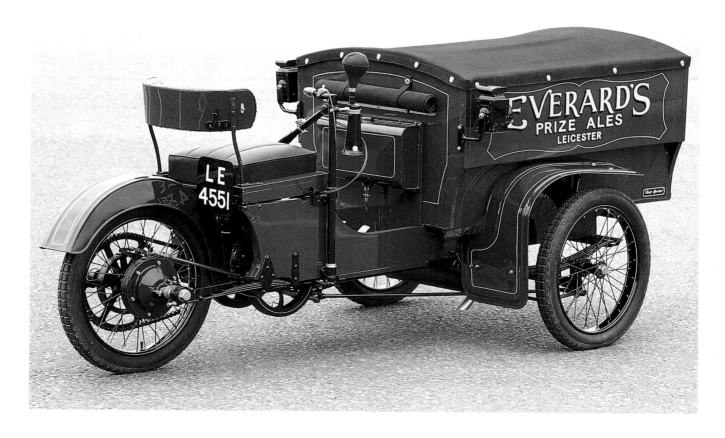

This superbly restored Auto-Carrier is in the National Motorcycle Museum just outside Birmingham. The single-cylinder engine lives under the seat, cooled by twin fans that are turned by contact with twin flywheels. Steering is by tiller, and the two-speed epicyclic gearbox is controlled by lever and pedal

Soames Langton demonstrates that getting the maximum out of a Sociable requires courage, co-ordination and a sense of humour. Catalogued optional equipment included hood (£5 5s), front wheel brakes (£3 3s) and a gong to warn of your impending approach

THE EDGE ERA

A s soon as the war was over John Weller was ready with his great contribution to the history of car design: an advanced small six-cylinder engine, with overhead camshaft and the block, pistons and sump cast in alloy. The first units, developing 40 bhp, were running in 1919. (The last, developing 105 bhp, were made in 1963, a record-setting production span of 44 years.)

Initially the engine was of only 1477 cc, but the bore was soon increased to give 1991 cc. The camshaft was driven by a long chain, held in tension by an ingenious spring-steel slipper device which, patented by Weller, has been widely used by others ever since.

As well as the Light Six, the other great influence in the 1920s was the powerful figure of Selwyn Francis Edge. S.F.Edge had been a prominent racing driver of Napiers during the Edwardian era, winning the Gordon Bennet Cup in 1902 and setting a 24-hour single-handed record at Brooklands in 1907, and he was a fervent believer in the publicity that accrued from competition success. He fell out with Napier in 1913, and his lucrative termination agreement with them shut him out of the motor industry

until 1921, when he bought himself onto the board of AC and was appointed Governing Director. His autocratic personality did not endear him to Portwine and Weller, who were gone from the company they had founded within a year.

It took some time to productionise the six-cylinder, and the majority of the early post-war cars used the humbler side-valve Anzani four-cylinder. But they were beautifully made, usually wearing simple but elegant two-seater touring and sports bodies. Despite a 1922 price of £575, £200 more than a Morris Cowley, they started to sell well with a reputation for quality and good handling.

Edge's publicity-seeking competition policy helped, too, with a determined programme of racing and record-breaking. In 1922, with a four-cylinder version of the overhead-cam engine, an AC was the first 1500 cc car to cover 100 miles in under an hour. Using the six, Tom Gillett set a new 24-hour record at over 82 mph in 1924, and in 1926 the Hon Victor Bruce and William Brunell scored the first Monte Carlo Rally victory for a British car. The next year Bruce, his wife Mildred and J.A.Joyce achieved 15,000 miles round the French Montlhéry track in nine days.

But other manufacturers' products were growing up fast. While the alloy six grew smoother thanks to a fifth main bearing and a crankshaft damper, chassis-wise the production cars were developed little. The rear-mounted gearbox was still restricted to three speeds, and front-wheel brakes remained an extra until the end of 1926 — at which time the fuel tank over the passengers' knees, with its dashboard filler, was finally moved to the rear of the car. A 1.5-litre narrow-bore version of the six was catalogued, although few if any were sold, and a freewheel was offered as a £20 option to counteract criticisms of a noisy gearbox.

Wheelbases got longer and chassis got heavier, but sales continued to slow, and Edge had to invest more personal capital to keep things afloat. At the 1929 Motor Show the wire-wheeled Magna series brought in half-elliptic front springs to replace the quarter-elliptics, which were said to contribute to poor braking performance, but it was too late. The firm struggled on until early 1930 when, against the background of the deepening international recession, it was forced into liquidation, and Edge retired a disappointed and poorer man.

At that time scores of other small car manufacturers were meeting a similar fate, never to return. But AC's extraordinary ability to survive was about to be demonstrated.

The 12/24 four-cylinder used the side-valve Anzani engine, and became quite a familiar sight on the roads in the early 1920s. This example belongs to David Meynell, and has the standard two-seater body with dickey

Colin Dunn's 12/24 Empire two-seater is
regularly taken on Continental jaunts,
although in wet weather and modern traffic
the two-wheel brakes and beaded-edge tyres
demand the driver's full attention. Colin is
the second owner. The first had the car for
67 years, taking it with him when he emi-
grated from Yorkshire to Arizona. The fuel
tank is over the passengers' legs, and is filled
via the cap on the left of the dashboard

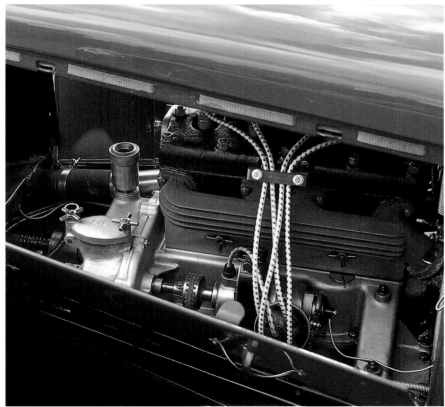

THIS PAGE AND PREVIOUS PAGES *The rakish 12/40 four-cylinder sports model came with a guarantee of 70 mph over the half-mile at Brooklands — if the new owner was prepared to pay extra for the cost of the certificate. This car, one of only two left in the world, has just returned to Britain after a long rebuild in Canada. Like all 1920s ACs, it has the controversial three-speed gearbox in unit with the back axle: the central disc is the handbrake*

This 1925 16 hp two-seater is a fine example of John Weller's six-cylinder in its first generation. David Wakefield has owned it for 25 years: in the 1960s the previous owner, a doctor, was still using it on his rounds in Stoke-on-Trent. From new it would have had rear-wheel brakes only, but in 1927 it was returned to the factory for front brakes to be added. It has the single Solex updraught carburettor: the chain-drive for the camshaft is at the back of the engine, with the water pump driven off the front

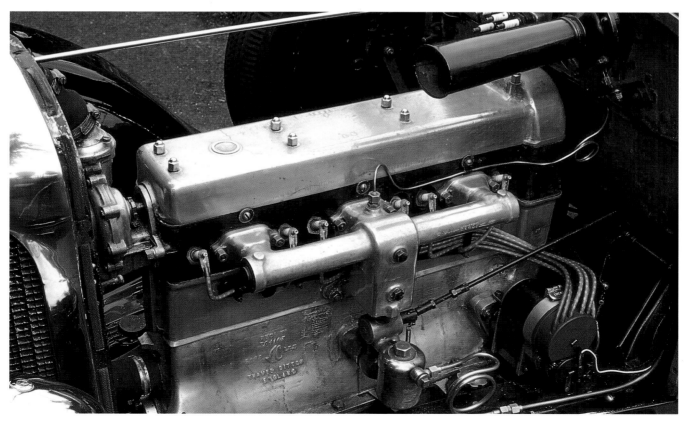

The body is simple but well-finished. Gear-lever and handbrake are on the right. The rear-mounted gearbox gives a flat floor, but leg-room in the dickey is limited. The ingenious device below takes warm air from the exhaust manifold through the block to the carburettor

David Hescroff's Montlhéry has a unique history. In 1930 Ray Morley, already an active competitions driver, bought enough parts from the bankrupt factory to make himself a successful six-cylinder trials and rally mount. The body came from the car used in 1927 by the Bruces and J.A. Joyce to set the 15,000-mile Montlhéry record, complete with single-seater dickey which is occupied here by Jonathan Burn, son of photographer Peter

THE HURLOCK FAMILY

IN 1930 THE OFFICIAL RECEIVER sold off the remains of the AC company. Cars were no longer being made, but a lot of spare parts were left in the almost empty factory, and some of the original work-force were still employed servicing customers' cars.

All of this was of interest to William and Charles Hurlock, two car dealer brothers who were running a booming truck, car ·hire, motor spares and road haulage firm in South London. They bought AC for its profitable servicing business, and because they needed more space for

building and repairing truck bodies: they had no intention of becoming car manufacturers.

But the spirit of AC refused to die. When William Hurlock wanted a new car, the service manager offered to build him up a Light Magna saloon out of existing parts. Faithful AC owners asked for replacements, and a few more were built to special order. By 1932 the stocks of parts were running low, and the Hurlocks bowed to the demand and went into production with an attractive new car on a 9ft 4ins chassis bought-in from Standard – and

using, at last, a conventional ENV four-speed gearbox.

The Hurlock brothers enjoyed rallying their cars, and in the 1933 RAC Rally four ACs were entered: Charles finished 4th, William was 6th, but the outright winner was Kitty Brunell, daughter of Bruce's 1926 Monte Carlo co-driver. The fourth car, a drophead coupé, won the *concours d'elegance* at the end of the rally.

In October 1933 AC Cars were back at the London Motor Show, after a four-year gap, with five cars on the stand. All used a new 9ft 7ins underslung chassis and all were rakish and good-looking, painted in differing shades of grey: a four-seater tourer, a coupé, two styles of drophead and a pillarless four-door saloon. There was also a bare chassis to invite the attention of outside coach-builders who may have been interested.

Of course the engine continued to be John Weller's Light Six, in 16/56 or three-carburettor 16/66 tune. Assembly and detail finish were to the highest standard. This helped to justify prices from £435 for the drophead to £495 for the Ace coupé, at a time when Bill Lyons' new SS – which used the same Standard chassis – was two-thirds the price.

By 1935 the rounded nose had given way to a handsome flat radiator, with mesh grille: a year later came the definitive slatted radiator. The various body styles – saloons, dropheads, tourers, coupés, all made by hand and few completely identical – were the epitome of under-stated 1930s elegance. Equipment included built-in jacks, automatic chassis lubrication and Telecontrol adjustable shock-absorbers.

The first Hurlock cars had a round-fronted radiator, and a proper four-speed gearbox at last, but had not yet adopted the lower underslung chassis. This is Bob Marsden's 1933 16/66 sports four-seater, one of the earliest of the new era. A similar car won the RAC Rally that year. The traditional AC attributes of elegant simplicity and quality finish had evidently survived the takeover intact

At the 1935 show the short-chassis two-seater appeared, on an 8ft 10ins wheelbase, with twin spare wheels mounted on a slab tank at the rear, flared scuttle and cutaway doors. *Autocar* tested it to an 85 mph maximum, with 50 mph in second gear. The three-carb engine was now rated at 16/70, for 70 bhp, and was followed by the 16/80 using a higher-compression head with bigger valves. A supercharged version later became available, called the 16/90. The ENV crash gearbox had been replaced by a choice of Moss synchro box or ENV preselector.

As always the clientele attracted to AC was discerning, but small. Sales were never brisk, and in the nine years since the Hurlock takeover fewer than 700 cars had been built. As war clouds gathered over Europe, the Hurlocks were already boosting turnover with component work sub-contracted from the aircraft industry, as well as building fire pumps and hose-laying equipment.

Their last pre-war car was an ill-judged attempt at modernity, a heavier, softer saloon with bulbous wings, which was consigned to oblivion in 1939 when war stopped car production altogether. From then on at Thames Ditton it was guns, fire engines, aircraft wing assemblies, missiles and flame-throwers.

In 66 bhp form, Weller's engine boasted three sidedraught SUs. The ENV crash box was operated by a neat remote lever, with guard for reverse

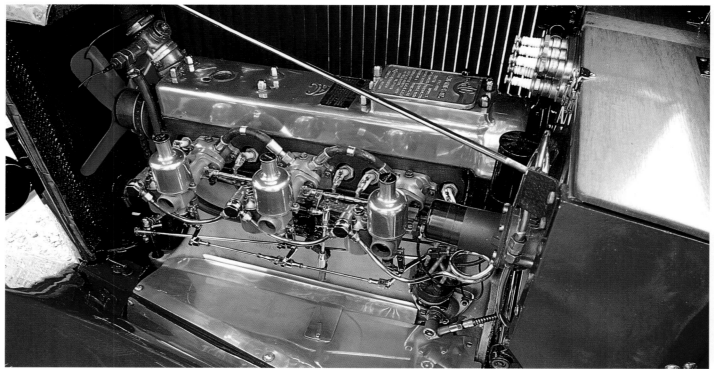

In 1934 Autocar *commented that AC enjoyed a following "attracted in the first instance by the pleasing lines of the car and by the comfort and convenience of the coachwork". The 16/66 undoubtedly lived up to the marque's reputation*

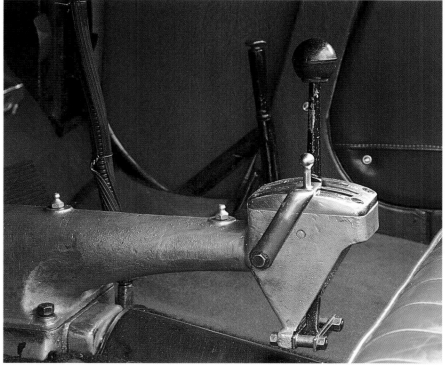

OPPOSITE *Bernard Driver's drophead left the factory in 1935, with attractive and comfortable two-door coachwork plus dickey. The new, flatter radiator used a mesh grille at this stage*

ABOVE AND RIGHT *One of the most charming factory bodies was the 2-4-6 coupé, so named because it could carry two passengers in the front, two on a hammock back seat that could be rolled up to admit more luggage, and two in the dickey. Brian Stannah's 1939 example, however, dispensed with the dickey and had a top-hinged conventional boot instead*

Perhaps the most elegant of all pre-war ACs is the March tourer, an open four-seater on the 9 ft 7 ins wheelbase. David Hescroff's lovely black example shows the 1930s sunburst styling of the door trim, the black-enamelled carburettor bodies and the well-stocked dash, with two gauges for front and rear Telecontrol shock absorbers in front of the passenger. (See title page)

THESE PAGES AND PREVIOUS PAGE *John Esher's 1937 Greyhound uses the optional wider-track chassis and is a commodious coachbuilt five-seater saloon. Yet weight was kept below 25 cwt, and 75 mph was possible. AC offered their customers any choice of colour, and the lines suit two-tone paintwork particularly well*

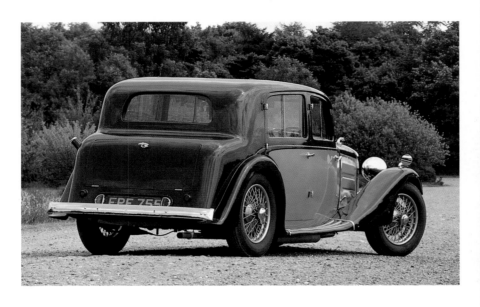

In 1935 a two-seater chassis on an 8 ft 10 ins chassis was produced, with engine output increased to 80 bhp thanks to a new cylinder head with larger valves. This was the birth of the classic 16/80. DPD 40 was Thames Ditton's first demonstrator and went on to have a distinguished trials and rally career: it now belongs to David Hescroff

During its four-year life the 16/80 appeared in basically two forms, and David Hescroff's examples of each allow comparison. The silver car dates from 1936 and shows the flared scuttle and slab rear fuel tank with twin spare wheels, while the white one is two years younger and has a slightly higher bonnet line, flat scuttle, disappearing hood and rounded tail. EPJ 101 is the famous car in which the redoubtable Betty Haig won the 2-litre class in the 1946 Alpine Trial when the car was already 10 years old

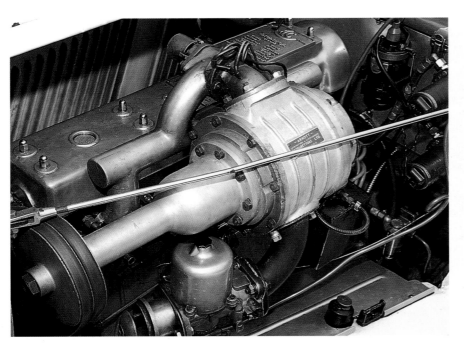

The dash on the flared-scuttle cars was painted body colour, while on the later ones it was trimmed to match the seats. For an extra £35 the 16/80 was also available with an Arnott supercharger, driven by a belt from the front of the crankshaft. In this guise it was called the 16/90. GPH 486 is one of these rare beasts, but the only external clue is a tiny bulge in the bonnet to clear the pulley.

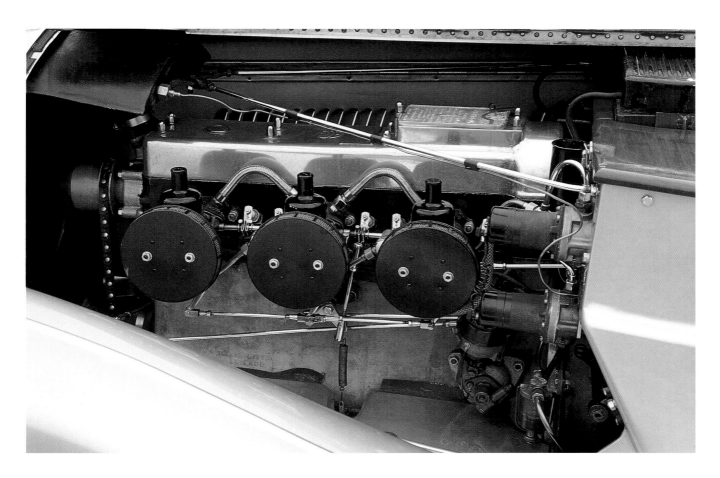

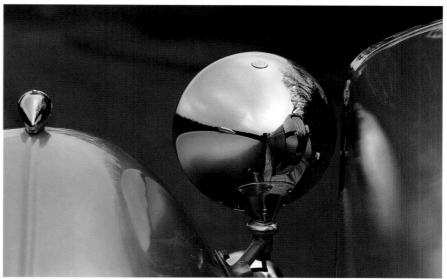

When Autocar road-tested the 16/80 they achieved a genuine 90mph with the windscreen folded flat. Motor found it "glued to the road as if on rails and delightful to handle: it enables one to recapture to the full the real joy and spirit of motoring"

POST-WAR RESPECTABILITY

WITH THE COMING OF PEACE and the period of austerity that accompanied it, the Hurlocks decided to adopt a single-model policy, and a conservative one at that. Their new Two Litre used as always the Weller overhead-cam engine, now producing a reliable 74 bhp, in a traditional leaf-sprung chassis clothed with a commodious aluminium two-door saloon body on a traditional wooden frame. The styling, with waterfall grille and tunnelled headlights, contrived to look sober and restrained but at the same time quite dashing for its day, although at 26 cwt the performance was not particularly sporting. Under road test conditions maximum speed was just shy of 80 mph.

At the 1949 Earls Court Motor Show, by which time the Two Litre had been in production for almost two years, the UK price including purchase tax

In the austere days after the war, AC's new Two Litre saloon was rather dashing. Colin Dunn is only the second owner of this immaculate 1951 example, but it was dismantled in 1959 for body repairs that were never done, and was in a bad state when he bought it. The car is still used for long journeys

was £1277, almost identical to the Armstrong Siddeley Typhoon, the faster but cruder Allard saloon, and the dated Alvis and Lea Francis 14s. But the stylish Riley saloon was definitely faster and £40 cheaper; and, as always, the Jaguar Mk V looked dangerously good value at the same money.

Three years further on, as other manufacturers developed more modern machinery, the AC was looking very old-fashioned. The price had gone up to £1600, £113 more than the new Rover 75 and £253 more than the Sunbeam-Talbot 90 – and for only £175 more you could get into the impressive new Mk VII Jaguar.

However, in Thames Ditton terms the Two Litre was a successful car. Once production of the new generation of sports cars got under way in 1954 it was only made to special order, but by the time the last one left the works in 1958 1129 had been built.

This number includes about 75 examples of the attractive four-seater tourer known as the Buckland, bodywork for which was sub-contracted to the Buckland Body Works of Buntingford in Herts. This appeared with both cutaway and straight-topped doors, initially with sidescreens and latterly with wind-up Perspex windows. The Buckland was lighter than the saloon, and with its flat screen folded could approach 90 mph.

Towards the end of the model's life a four-door version appeared, and over 20 of these were made. There were also perhaps a dozen rather elegant drophead Two Litres, most with a traditional exposed pram-iron hood, but some with a rear quarter-light and hidden arms, and one or two with fixed window rails and a cabriolet hood arrangement. A small handful of chassis were sold to provincial coachbuilders to be bodied as ungainly shooting brakes, to take advantage of purchase tax concessions then available on this type of body.

TOP *The 2-litre's big body provided armchair comfort, with a simple central dash. More sporting was the Buckland tourer (opposite above), with fold-flat screen and 90 mph potential. Mike Beresford's handsome four-door saloon (opposite below) is one of about two dozen made*

The rarest Two Litre is the drophead coupé. Ros Claydon's husband gave her this one-owner
car as a 40th birthday present: like her, it was born in 1948. It is very original and, apart
from a new hood, has never been restored

THE ACE, AND GLORY

SCATTERED THROUGH THE HISTORY of the motor-car are all manner of chance meetings and happy coincidences, and the AC story is no exception. By the mid-1950s William Hurlock was approaching retirement, but his son Derek had joined Charles to help run the company. The Two Litre was clearly outdated: developing a modern new model would require great investment, and the Hurlocks doubted whether their small family concern could compete with the big manufacturers.

Meanwhile, the shop next-door to Bucklands at Buntingford, where the Two Litre tourers were bodied, was being rented by a clever young racing car builder of Portuguese extraction called John Tojeiro. His lightweight two-seaters, with simple twin-tube frame and all-independent transverse-leaf suspension, were regular class winners in British sports-car racing.

Tojeiro only made the chassis: choice of engine was up to the customer, and for the body some went to a little works in Hammersmith, where Eric Gray could turn out a very neat copy of the pretty Ferrari 166 Barchetta bodyshell. Tojeiro's landlord, a local garage

---

BELOW *Tom McWhirter's jewel-like AC-engined Ace was the very last one sold. It was delivered in August 1963, by which time Thames Ditton were concentrating on Cobras*

owner called Vin Davison, had built up a Lea-Francis-engined version, and in the summer of 1953 Bucklands' boss Ernie Bailey suggested he show it to the Hurlocks.

The rest, as they say, is history. AC not only bought Vin Davison's car on the spot, but also hired him to develop it into a production car. They paid Tojeiro for the design rights, and agreed a royalty of £5 per car for the first 100 units. Three months later Davison's racer was on the AC stand at Earls Court as the new AC Ace, now with quality paintwork, properly upholstered and trimmed, and with chrome wire wheels and windscreen. Under the bonnet, needless to say, was John Weller's Light Six, now developing 85 bhp.

It took until the middle of 1954 for the production version to appear, with a subtly strengthened chassis,

minor body modifications and AC's usual attention to detail and quality. But it still only weighed 16.5 cwt, and could easily top 100 mph. More significant were the superb roadholding and handling, which set new standards at a time when no other British sportscar had all-independent suspension. And everyone agreed that the car had a visual grace and purity better even than the Ferrari that had been its unknowing progenitor.

Almost at once the Ace started to make its name in

ABOVE *David Wakefield's 1954 Ace was the 12th production car. It has the early circular tail lights (the reflectors are a later addition) and is a "long boot" car — the boot lid reaches forward almost to the edge of the cockpit, which results in a rather abrupt hood line. This was shortened on later cars*

RIGHT *The big air intake on the standard Ace, like David Boland's on the left, was not aerodynamically ideal, so for competition work AC offered an alloy cowl to improve penetration. It was said to add 3 mph top speed — more if, like Tony Bancroft's, it was in race trim with aero screen. With the shorter-stroke 2.6 Ford engine a lower bonnet line was possible, like on David Sanderson's Ace 2.6 on the right. This was carried through unchanged for the Mk I Cobra. The flat windscreen, as on David B's car, was standard; the curved screen, as on David S's, was a factory extra*

racing and rallying, in Britain, Europe and the USA. One of its most prominent drivers was Sussex motor dealer Ken Rudd, who in the quest for more power fitted his Ace with a Bristol engine. With its iron block and downdraught carburettors this BMW-based two-litre six was heavier and taller than the elderly AC engine, but it breathed much better, and its crossover pushrod valve gear could cope with higher revs. Even in road trim it developed 20 bhp more and was good for almost 120 mph; when tuned for racing, up to 150 bhp and 130 mph were possible.

By 1957 the Ace-Bristol was in production in 120 bhp form at a hefty £2011, against the £1651 of the AC-engined version. For comparison, the MGA cost £961, the Triumph TR3 £1021, the big Austin-Healey £1144 and the Jaguar XK140 £1693. Of them all, the Ace was the truest sports car: it could be used for daily commuting or for high-speed long-distance touring, but it could also be driven to a race meeting, campaigned with distinction, and driven home again — even if that race meeting was the Le Mans 24 Hours.

Between 1954 and 1963 a total of 723 Aces were sold, over 500 of them for export. More than half had Bristol engines, but in 1961 Bristol switched to Chrysler V8 power for their own cars, and stopped making the six-cylinder unit.

Once again Ken Rudd came to Thames Ditton's rescue by proposing the 2.6-litre Ford Zephyr engine. When fitted with Raymond Mays 12-port alloy head and Weber carburettors this could be made to produce a torquey 170 bhp. It was slightly heavier, but its short-stroke design made it more compact, so AC took the opportunity to lower the nose and bonnet line, thus producing the Ace 2.6, which for many is the prettiest Ace of all. It is also the rarest: only 37 were built before another significant meeting changed the course of AC history once more.

ABOVE *The Ace's lithe body shape was based on the Tojeiro sports-racer, and thus in turn on the Ferrari Barchetta. Shivering in the Yorkshire dawn are, left to right, David Boland, David Sanderson and Tony Bancroft*

LEFT *Ace suspension joints and bushes need frequent greasing, so grease gun and oil can were mounted accessibly under the bonnet. This is David Wakefield's early car*

ABOVE *David Boland's boot shows correct plain finish: the leather loop is to hold the hood sticks*

BELOW *This Sanderson Ace has unique cowls on speedo and rev-counter, fitted by the factory at the request of the original owner*

LEFT *The long-nosed Ace 2.6 has surely one of the purest shapes of any post-war sports car. Only 37 were made. As an undergraduate in 1965, Simon Taylor bought his 2.6 third-hand for £650. He sold it three years later — and then spent 24 years trying to buy it back, before it returned to his garage in 1992 after a long sojourn in the Far East*

BELOW LEFT *David Boland's Ace, a typically flawless Sanderson rebuild, displays the correct cockpit trim with hip-hugging bucket seats, big fly-off handbrake, alloy-spoked wood-rim wheel (a factory extra) and long cranked gearlever*

BELOW *The factory hardtop was of fibreglass. This view of Tony Bancroft's 1957 car also shows the competition modifications — short exhaust, hot air exit in the wing and cold air scoop on the bonnet — which helped to make well-prepared Ace-Bristols unbeatable in their class in 1950s club racing*

RIGHT AND OPPOSITE, TOP *When the Bristol engine went out of production in 1961, AC fitted the 2.6-litre Ford Zephyr engine to 37 Aces. Ken Rudd initiated this project, and the cars had RS chassis numbers, for Ruddspeed. Usually the 12-port alloy Raymond Mays cylinder head was fitted, with lightweight pistons and pushrods. This engine produced 155 bhp using three SU carburettors (Stage 3), and a claimed 170 bhp on triple twin-choke Webers (Stage 4). Simon Bathurst-Brown owns the first Ace 2.6, built up on a standard-nosed chassis by Ken Rudd, which is in Stage 4 tune*

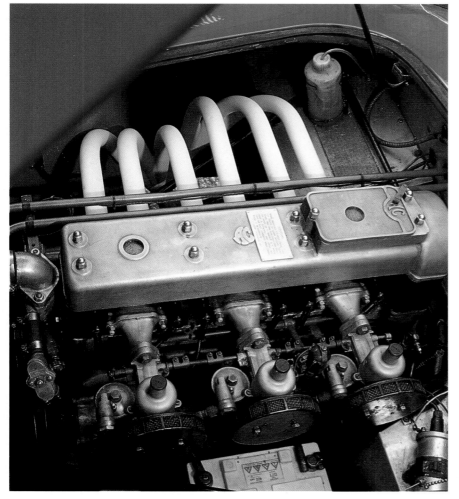

OPPOSITE, BELOW *Of the 723 AC Aces built, 223 used the traditional single-cam six, seen here in David Wakefield's car. Basically unchanged since Weller designed it, and still using the three SUs of the 16/80s, it now had the water pump mounted on the side of the block to lower its height. It produced 85 bhp in the early Aces, and up to 105 bhp with nitrided crank in its final form*

LEFT *The Bristol engine was fitted to 463 cars, usually in 100D2 form developing 128 bhp, although race-prepared units produced 140 bhp or more. Tony Bancroft's has had the air cleaners atop the Solex downdraught carburettors replaced with air-splitters, as often fitted to racing Bristol engines*

LEFT *A line-up of Aces at Waddesdon Manor, with Simon Taylor's 2.6 heading the queue. In 1959 the third car along, in pale green, was a standard secondhand Ace-Bristol that belonged to a lady customer of Ken Rudd's. It was borrowed for the second week of June and driven to Le Mans, where it was entered in the 24-hour race. It finished seventh overall and won the 2-litre class in the hands of Ted Whiteaway and Jack Turner, and was then driven home again and returned to its owner. It now belongs to John Deveson*

ABOVE *The Ace dash is simple and clear, with big five-inch speedo and rev-counter. The twin tubes above the transmission tunnel run in a tall triangle from chassis frame to scuttle to stiffen the structure*

LEFT AND BELOW *A stone bothy in the wilds of Aberdeenshire is hardly where you'd expect to find a collection of unique ACs. Barrie Bird's garage houses five Thames Ditton products, including two one-off Le Mans cars in the works' colours of pale metallic green. The naked frame is that of Ace chassis number AE22 - the second production Ace built, which Barrie is restoring. Beneath the tubes that support the body, the Ace's sturdy ladder frame can be seen, with the mounting for the differential at the back*

BOTTOM *Using the chassis number LM5000, AC built this sports-racing prototype in 1958 for the Le Mans 24 Hour race. Despite very little development, it was driven by Peter Bolton and Dick Stoop into eighth place, and was timed at 154 mph on the Mulsanne Straight*

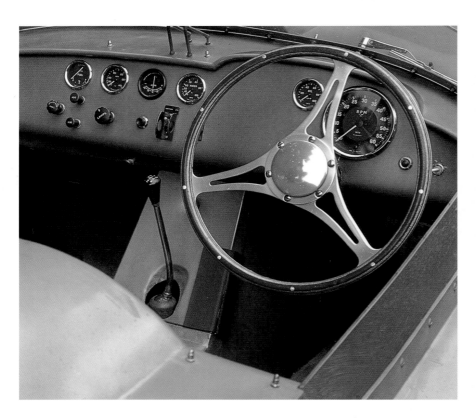

LM5000 marked a brief renewal of AC's relationship with John Tojeiro, as he designed its multi-tubular spaceframe, and Cavendish Morton's svelte body shape was also close to his work on the Tojeiro racers. The engine was Bristol, of course, and suspension was by coils and wishbones at the front, with a swing axle/coil arrangement at the rear. Since the 1960s Barrie Bird has preserved this unique and historic car in exactly its Le Mans form — down to the same racing number, 28

GRAN TURISMO

THE YEAR AFTER THE PROTOTYPE ACE made its bow at Earls Court, the AC stand had another newcomer, a beautiful little fastback coupé version called the Aceca. With wind-up windows, a big luggage area and better sound insulation, it rivalled the most exotic Italian GTs, and at a price by 1957 of £2063 it was more affordable. It was only slightly heavier than the Ace, so its performance was little different, and it too became available with the Bristol engine. In all, 328 Acecas were built, split roughly equally between Bristol- and AC-engined versions, and almost half of these went for export. There were also eight Zephyr-engined cars, although unlike the Ace 2.6, their bonnet line and grille remained unchanged.

The Aceca's popularity produced a demand for a full four-seater version, but different suspension would be

ABOVE *Graham Murrell's Aceca-Bristol displays its opening rear window, which predated the popular hatchback but did not initiate this feature in GT terms (the Aston-Martin DB2/4 beat it by 12 months). The window was of glass on the prototype, but perspex thereafter*

LEFT *If the Ace was the prettiest 1950s sports car, the Aceca can lay claim to being the prettiest GT. Angus Ridgwell is another who has owned his AC twice: he bought it new in 1961, sold it after 80,000 miles, and then found it by chance 16 years later as a wreck. That was in 1982, and after a six-year rebuild it became one of the best Acecas in existence. Both Graham and Angus have replaced the correct narrow 16-inch wheels, for which tyres are now hard to find, with wider 72-spoke 15-inch wheels*

needed to allow the engine to move forward and the rear bulkhead back. For some time AC experimented with a couple of enlarged Acecas, one using a flat-six 2-litre engine, before the prototype Greyhound appeared at the 1959 London Show. The lengthened twin-tube chassis had coil suspension all round, using wishbones at the front and trailing links at the rear, but almost a year passed before it went into production with a new square-tube frame and tidier styling.

Like all ACs it was beautifully made in the traditional manner, with an elegant fastback body enclosing seating for four adults in a cockpit awash with luxurious fine leather and walnut. But perhaps the rear suspension geometry needed more development, for road testers spoke of nervous handling and sudden oversteer. Only 82 were built: with a torquier 2.2-litre version of the Bristol engine it cost £3089, although AC and occasionally Zephyr engines were also fitted before the last one was made at the end of 1961.

The Aceca had a luxurious interior, with a completely different dashboard from the Ace. There was a binnacle for the main instruments in front of the driver, and walnut as well as leather. Beneath the tailgate the carpeted boot would swallow a lot of luggage. There was no effort to supply occasional seats. Under Angus Ridgwell's care, the AC engine becomes a thing of polished beauty

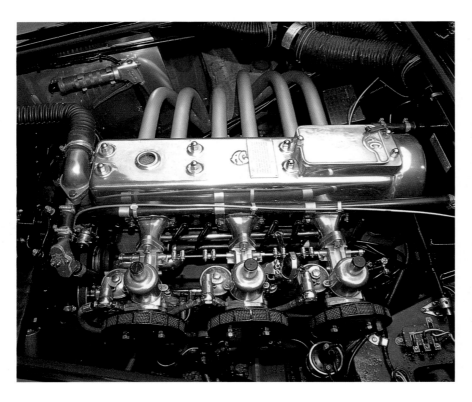

Simon Bathurst-Brown's Greyhound shows how the Aceca's lines were successfully translated into a larger car, with interior finish and equipment that equalled any of the luxury GTs of the day. The rear seat was large enough, and low enough, for two adults to be accommodated in reasonable comfort. The boot lid was hinged at the bottom, so that oversize luggage could be carried with the boot open

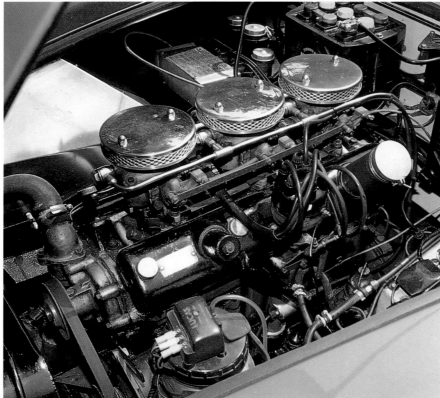

AC's artistry with aluminium was evident in the sweep of the Greyhound's rear quarters and in the subtle peak around the headlights. The Bristol engine was usual Greyhound wear, sometimes in torquier 2.2-litre form to deal with the extra weight

THE MAN FROM TEXAS

LET'S ADMIT ONE THING STRAIGHT AWAY: putting a lightweight cast-iron Ford V8 into an AC Ace was Carroll Shelby's idea. But if you believe all the hype that has surrounded the Cobra over the past 30 years, most of it emanating from North America, you might think that Thames Ditton played no part at all in the making of this Sixties icon.

However, when Shelby knocked on AC's door in the autumn of 1961 it was an even greater stroke of good fortune for the Hurlocks than Ernie Bailey's introduction to the Tojeiro chassis eight years before. Having retired from racing after a strong international career that included winning Le Mans for Aston Martin, this rangy Texan nursed an ambition to sell a sports car in the US that combined V8 power with European style and handling. He had a contact at Ford in Detroit who lent him two of their new thinwall-cast V8s and, after preliminary discussions with the Hurlocks, one was flown to Thames Ditton.

Over that winter Vin Davison and chief designer Alan Turner worked to fit it in a modified chassis. They found it was lighter than the Zephyr unit, but its much greater power potential called for heavier gauge tubing, extra bracing and a heftier Salisbury diff. The Ace 2.6 body was used almost unchanged, but with the wheel openings flared slightly to cover fatter wheels and a wider track.

The AC Cobra may have mixed parentage – Tojeiro, Thames Ditton, Shelby and Detroit - but it became one of the great cars of all time. It is interesting to speculate about a slightly different parentage: Shelby had actually approached Chevrolet for an engine early on

The resulting confection weighed just 1.5 cwt more than the Ace-Bristol, but had double the power and double the torque. Not surprisingly the performance – 0-60 in 4.4 secs and 0-100 in under 12 secs – was entirely in a class of its own, but the Tojeiro-based chassis still coped with it pretty well.

Helped by Shelby's extrovert character and instant competition results in the USA, the Cobra (the name came to Shelby in a dream) became a sensation. At first it was for America only: AC sent engineless cars to California for Shelby to finish off, initially with 4.2-litre (260 cu.in) and then, as the Mk II, with 4.7-litre (289 cu.in) engines. During 1963 the Ace's Bishop cam steering gear was replaced by rack and pinion, and later that year the first fully-assembled right-hand-drive cars became available from Thames Ditton. In all, just 61 European-spec Mk II Cobras were built, the remainder of the total of 655 leaf-spring cars going to the USA.

Not content with dominating national racing in the USA, Shelby – strongly encouraged behind the scenes by Ford in Detroit – wanted to win on the world stage. So Cobras ran in most of the classic endurance races in 1963, supplemented from the start of the 1964 season at Daytona by an aerodynamic coupé designed in California by Pete Brock. It was known thereafter as the Daytona Cobra and six were built, and with a mixture of these and the roadsters the Shelby team beat Ferrari to win the 1965 World GT Championship.

But Shelby wanted even more power, and had been experimenting with the 427 cu.in (7-litre) Ford V8, which could produce up to 400 bhp and beyond. A more rigid chassis was badly needed, and with help from Ford's engineers the Mk III appeared, with thicker, wider-based tubing and coil/wishbone suspension finally replacing the

transverse leaf set-up that dated back to John Tojeiro. Wheels were fatter still and bodywork was wider and more flared, with a bigger radiator intake. Homologation difficulties and the march of the rear-engined GT40s and Ferraris kept the Mk III from international success, but it was a formidable weapon in American national racing.

Shelby sold Mk IIIs in street, competition and semi-competition (S/C) forms, the latter made up of 31 unsold competition cars that were slightly detuned for electrifying road use. One road test of a street version recorded 0-100 in 8.8 secs and a top speed of 165 mph. This was with the correct high-performance 427 mill: some street cars used the softer 428 cu.in engine, which had a narrower bore/longer stroke and hydraulic lifters.

Colin Sanders' late Mk II has amber front indicators and Mk III-type rear lights, but is in precisely the form in which it left the factory as one of only 42 right-hand drive Mk IIs for the British market. Apart from the wheel arch flares, the body is unchanged from the Ace 2.6, although there are more substantial horizontal bumpers, hot air exits in the front wings, side deflectors on the windscreen and a central fuel filler. (The impact of the Cobra in competition was huge: in 1964, Ferrari demanded that their 250LM and 275LM be homologated for the Coppa d'Europa to see off the foreign threat to 'their' race. When this was refused, the organisers at Monza cancelled the race!)

Thames Ditton supplied over 300 chassis to Shelby during 1965 and 1966, and in 1966 started a small series of European Mk IIIs, using the 4.7-litre engine. During the next couple of years only 27 were sold, 20 of them on the home market. As Ford now owned the Cobra name they were called AC 289s.

In all, over a seven-year period, less than 1000 Cobras were built. But so great is the Cobra's grip on the imagination of enthusiasts all over the world that, as the prices of genuine cars soared, so more replicas, forgeries and kit-car copies have appeared than of any other car. And it can all be traced back to Vin Davison's 1953 Tojeiro special ...

ABOVE AND RIGHT *David Hescroff's maroon Mk II, originally the works demonstrator, is a delightfully original, well-used car which he has owned for 15 years. In contrast to the Ace dash, there is an oil temperature gauge, twist-key starter, and central clock*

LEFT *Colin Sanders' car shows how the 4.7-litre V8 sits well back in the chassis. Weight distribution is 49 per cent front, 51 percent rear*

LEFT *The Mk I Cobras, which used the slightly smaller 4.2-litre V8, all went to the USA apart from one demonstrator which was retained by the factory. But Ashley Bird's Mk I was reimported in 1974 and converted to right-hand drive, and is now powered by the first engine that Shelby sent over to Thames Ditton in 1961. Like all Mk Is it has Ace-type Bishop Cam steering rather than the rack and pinion that was adopted after the first 51 Mk IIs had been built, identifiable by the Ace-type steering wheel*

ABOVE *Shelby man Pete Brock built the first Daytona coupé in 1964, and five more were built using shells sub-contracted to Carrozzeria Gransport in Italy. They helped Shelby to beat Ferrari in the 1965 World GT Championship*

GPG 4C is one of the most illustrious of all Competition Mk II Cobras. It was raced in 1964
by Roy Salvadori and Chris Amon for its first owner, Tommy Atkins, and then in 1965/66 in
the white-with-black colours of The Chequered Flag by Roger Mac, Bob Bondurant, Roy Pike
and Mike Beckwith. Its competition career continued over a span of some 15 years, and its red
and gold livery dates from 1970 when Shaun Jackson scored ten wins in a season

The engine boasts Gurney-Weslake heads, downdraught Webers and 400 bhp, and on a sprint final drive ratio, 0-100mph occupies nine seconds

Simon Taylor tests GPG 4C on a rain-soaked track. As a proper Competition Mk II, it has cutaway trailing edges to the doors to clear the bigger rear wheel arches, jacking points instead of bumpers, Halibrand magnesium-alloy wheels, and extra ducting to get hot air away from the brakes

The Daytona coupé demonstrated the value of improving the Cobra's
aerodynamics, so Thames Ditton decided to build their own racing
Cobra coupé with a one-off body sub-contracted to Maurice Gomm,
using chassis number A98. They entered it for the 1964 Le Mans 24
Hours, having first unwittingly attracted adverse publicity by testing it
at dawn on the M1 at 183 mph. (It is hardly fair, however, to blame
this car for the imposition of the 70 mph limit the following year!) In
the race Peter Bolton and Jack Sears were seventh at the end of the
first hour, but during the night Bolton spun off when a tyre blew —
and then Baghetti's Ferrari crashed into the AC, destroying it and
killing three spectators who had got into a prohibited area. Many
years later the wreck was bought by Barrie Bird, who painstakingly
recreated A98 to exactly its correct form, using the original engine and
getting Maurice Gomm to make a new body on the original bucks

On the 30th anniversary of A98's disastrous 24 Hours outing, Barrie and June Bird drove the thunderous beast on the road from their home in Aberdeen to Le Mans, and did three laps of honour before the 1994 race began

The ultimate Cobra, the epitome of excess, macho horsepower, is the Mk III 427, whose shape has been copied by countless kitcar builders on both sides of the Atlantic. This superb example is one of the S/C cars with front oil cooler, side exhausts, riveted bonnet scoop and roll-over bar, and belongs to Udo Kruse

The S/C dash has rev-counter, oil pressure and water temperature gauges in front of the driver; items of lesser importance, like the speedometer, are in the centre. The side exhausts contain minimal integral silencers that do precious little silencing

Just 31 7-litre competition cars were sold for road use as S/C (semi-competition or street-competition) Mk IIIs, and genuine examples of these are probably the most valuable Cobras of all. Despite all the copies and the forgeries, their brutal charisma remains undiminished

Nigel Dawes' Cobra Mk III is one of the rare European market 289s, with 4.7-litre V8, less extreme wheel arch flares and wire wheels. Only 20 right-hand drive cars were ever built

The smaller-engined coil-sprung Mk III is probably the most usable of all the Thames Ditton Cobras, lacking the brute force and huge tyres of the 7-litre cars, and being more refined than the leaf-sprung Mk II

ANGLO-ITALIAN

WHILE THE COBRA WAS DEFINITIVELY a pure sports car, Derek Hurlock realised that the coil-sprung chassis could be adapted to make a very fast luxury GT that combined Shelby performance with Italian styling and Thames Ditton finish. (Some years earlier a prototype drophead had been built on a leaf-spring chassis with the experimental flat-six engine: this still exists, but with a V8 installed). In 1965 a 427 chassis was lengthened by 6 ins and sent to the Turin coachbuilder Frua, who clothed it as a very handsome two-seater convertible in time for that year's Earls Court show. At Geneva the following spring there was a dramatic fastback coupé version.

The hydraulic-lifter 7-litre engine was used, which gave the car its name: 428. This made light work of the Fastback's 28 cwt, and even with automatic transmission

road test times of 0-60 in 5.9 secs and 0-100 in 14.5 secs were achievable, with a maximum over 140 mph. But at £5324 for the Convertible and £5573 for the Fastback it cost over £1000 more than a DB6 Aston Martin, or as much as two E-types and two Minis.

The real problem was with the supply and quality of the all-steel Frua bodies. These were mounted on rolling chassis sent out to Turin and then returned to Thames Ditton for painting and trimming, but Italian labour problems played havoc with delivery dates. In 1973, with the Middle East fuel crisis driving up the cost of running thirsty luxury cars, 428 production ended after 51 Fastbacks and 29 Convertibles had been built.

Louis Davidson's superb red Frua convertible was restored by Uniclip Automotive, which is run by Andy Shepherd, the AC Owners' Club 428 registrar. The body is steel and the chassis a six-inch longer version of the coil-sprung Mk III Cobra's; most had automatic transmission

The hydraulic-lifter 428 engine was more docile than the thunderous 427, but still gave the Frua-bodied car electrifying performance. Equipment was luxurious, and the majority had automatic transmission selected by a hefty U-bar lever. Frua's name appeared on the flanks of all 428s

The Fastback is a brutally elegant car with a 140 mph potential, and is visually even better balanced than the Convertible. Adrian Dawn's was the penultimate Fastback built

When 428 production ended, two interesting variants were under development, and both survive. The final Convertible had fold-away headlights, which modernised the frontal appearance considerably. And the last big Thames Ditton AC of all was an impressive four-seater coupé, a steel monocoque with power steering and, at first, de Dion rear suspension. For some years Derek Hurlock used it as his personal transport, and Brian Booth has been its only other owner. This unique car is now undergoing complete restoration

Six Cylinders Again

THE 1970S, WITH SOARING FUEL PRICES and inflation, were not a good time to be a luxury car manufacturer. Derek Hurlock decided that the way forward was to produce a smaller, more affordable sports GT, while still retaining the AC individuality and quality. Once again the obstacle was development costs, and once again he looked around for a John Tojeiro with an existing design that could be adapted.

This search led him to two young designers, Robin Stables and Peter Bohanna. At the 1973 Olympia Racing Car Show they had exhibited the Diablo, a prototype for a little coupé using a fabricated steel chassis and an Austin Maxi transverse power pack mounted over the rear wheels. AC bought the rights and set about developing it into a rapid two-seater GT. The little 1750 cc Maxi engine was not powerful enough, so a Ford 3-litre V6 was turned east-west and squeezed in: but this in turn required a stronger transmission, so a chain drive was developed using AC's own five-speed transaxle with Hewland gears.

A non-running mock-up appeared at the 1973 Earls Court Show, but development was very slow. For the next five years at show time the car, now called the ME 3000 (for mid-engined), was displayed, but no customer cars were delivered until 1979. In 1980 *Autocar* borrowed one for road test and found it brisk but not shatteringly fast by the standards of the day (0-60 in 8.5 secs, 120 mph). They liked its individual character, but strongly criticised its lift-off oversteer. At £13,300 it was £3300 more than a TVR 3000M and only £2800 less than a Porsche 911SC.

After just 71 had been made, production stopped at Thames Ditton. The project was sold to a new company, AC Cars (Scotland) Ltd, who built 30 more cars in Glasgow, including a prototype with an Alfa Romeo V6 engine. By 1985 they too were in trouble and, after resurfacing briefly as the Ecosse with Fiat power, the ME died.

LEFT *The ME 3000 has its own dedicated following, and many owners have continued developing the car's reliability and performance long after the model's demise*

Enthusiastic owners continued trying to sort out the snags, however. Several cars were turbo-charged for greater performance, and patient specialists demonstrated that the transmission reliability problems and tricky handling could be solved. In the 1990s the ME 3000 continues to have its keen supporters as a compact, rapid and entertaining road car in modern use.

ABOVE *Barrie Bird's ME, his everyday road car, has its sideways V6 in RS3100 tune to increase its Porsche-teasing potential*

LEFT *Pam Clark's immaculate ME demonstrates the model's compact dimensions. It is 13 ft 1 in long and 4 ft 1 in high, yet the cockpit is well-equipped and comfortable for two*

BACK TO ITS ROOTS

THAT AC SURVIVED AT THAMES DITTON as long as it did, when countless other specialised car manufacturers failed, was down to the Hurlock family's policy of diversification. At various times between 1933 and 1983 AC was losing money on every car it built, but other engineering work was paying the bills.

Look at the factory shots of the first Cobra, and you will see in the background rows and rows of golf club trolleys, called Bag Boys. The electric trains that used to carry holidaymakers along Southend Pier were entirely built by AC. So were a variety of trailers, truck bodies and airfield crash tenders, not to mention military and aeronautical contracts which continued after World War Two. And the most lucrative contract of all was with the Ministry of Pensions, later the Ministry of Health, to build many thousands of what were then ponderously called invalid carriages.

These three-wheelers, with the single wheel in front and handlebar steering, used an air-cooled single-cylinder engine, and were bodied initially in aluminium but subsequently in glassfibre. Primitive in the extreme, they were an ironic – and very profitable – flashback to the original Auto-Carrier and Sociable.

During the days of post-war austerity, with many people struggling to buy their first car, a two-seater version with conventional steering was introduced for normal sale. At first this was going to use a 350 cc Coventry Victor air-cooled twin and be bodied by Ernie Bailey as the Buckland Runabout, but it developed into the AC Petite with single-cylinder 350 cc Villiers two-stroke. At £362 (or £392 for the de luxe model, with bumpers, door locks and spare wheel), it was not a bargain when a new Ford Popular was

only £443, but a large number were built in the mid-1950s. The Suez crisis and petrol rationing of 1957 briefly produced a wider market for such economy cars, but they were killed off for ever by the advent of the Mini in 1959.

However, AC continued to be attracted by the city-car concept, and in the 1970s they built three- and four-wheeled prototypes which were evolved from the invalid car. But they could not be produced cheaply enough to be a viable alternative to the current mass-produced small saloons, and were shelved.

BELOW *Several generations of AC invalid car have been a familiar sight on our roads for 40 years. This is Joan Rabe's 1977 edition*

LEFT AND BELOW *The AC Petite, with 350 cc of two-stroke Villiers power, enjoyed a brief vogue in the 1950s, boasting conventional controls and room for two, or an adult and two children, on its bench seat. Alan Budd did his courting in a Petite, and has recently restored one of the very few remaining examples*

BELOW *AC experimented with three-and four-wheel versions of city cars in the early 1970s, but the project came to naught. The two prototypes now keep an Ace-Bristol and a Sociable company in the garage of AC Owners' Club chairman Brian Gilbart-Smith*

ENTER ANGLISS

IN 1979, DESPITE ITS OTHER ACTIVITIES, AC made a loss, which continued into the 1980s. For Derek Hurlock retirement beckoned, and the old factory in Thames Ditton High Street was sold for redevelopment.

But the myth and magic of the Cobra lived on. In the mid-1970s Brian Angliss was running Autokraft, a company specialising in the restoration of Cobras and the supply of unavailable parts. In 1982 he acquired most of the original tools and jigs from Thames Ditton, and the rights to the AC name in order to put the Cobra back into production.

This meant complying with modern regulations, particularly if the car was to be sold in the USA, and the result was the Cobra Mk IV, with federalised 5-litre Ford V8, roomier cockpit with modern switchgear, resited fuel tank and 5 mph bumpers. But it still looked very similar

to the Mk III of almost 20 years earlier — which, given these restrictions, was a considerable achievement. Around 480 were produced in the reborn AC Cars' spacious factory at Brooklands, on the site of the old track where ACs and others had campaigned in the 1920s. As with the original Cobras, large numbers went to the USA.

A lightweight Mk IV was also produced, with more traditional cockpit and dashboard and more highly tuned engine, which was even closer to the spirit and appearance of the original 427s. As always the standard of workmanship and execution on these latter-day ACs was superb: many of the old Thames Ditton craftsmen who worked on the Ace and the first Cobra now worked at Brooklands.

Sam and Linzi Smart are the AC Owners' Club Mk IV registrars, and Sam has been racing his 1987 example with success in inter-marque racing for several seasons. The car is always superbly turned out

But Angliss was looking beyond the Cobra to the next generation of ACs, and his close contacts with Ford produced a prototype Ace, using their V6 engine and four-wheel-drive, which was displayed on the Ford stand at the 1976 Motor Show. The following year Ford bought a controlling interest in AC, but the relationship with Angliss was never a happy one and, after much legal wrangling, Angliss got his independence back in 1992.

He persevered with the Ace through several prototypes until it appeared in its definitive version at the 1993 Motor Show, as a sports roadster with 5-litre Ford V8 power in a

BELOW *Both the Cobras in this picture date from the Angliss era: they are Mk IVs with the 5-litre 302 Mustang engine. The silver car is a Lightweight, and thus hard to distinguish from a Mark III. It belongs to Bob Glasspool. Next to it is a normal Mk IV with the longer nose and federal bumpers*

OPPOSITE *The Mk IV's dash in federalised form (below) is quite a surprise, with modern instruments and switchgear that can be traced back to humbler mass-production machinery. But if one comes up behind you on the road, this (above) will soon be the view you'll get*

stainless steel chassis. The luxurious alloy bodywork featured electric hood, air conditioning, heated seats and the rest, and Angliss said he was going straight for the Mercedes SL market – with a £50,000-plus price tag.

ABOVE AND OPPOSITE *The new AC Ace poses in front of the factory at Brooklands (top) and at the 1995 Detroit Motor Show. The cars are hand-built in the time-honoured AC way*

One of the stars of the 1995 Earls Court Motor Show, the new Ace has an all-alloy body and a chassis of stainless steel. The interior is luxurious in the modern supercar idiom, and under the bonnet is a fuel-injected 5-litre Ford V8. The AC badge lives on, 90 years after the Auto-Carrier

AC variety, spanning 50 years' production, on an Owners' Club event. A 1937 Greyhound saloon leads an ME 3000, an Aceca, a Mk IV and an Ace through the Derbyshire Dales

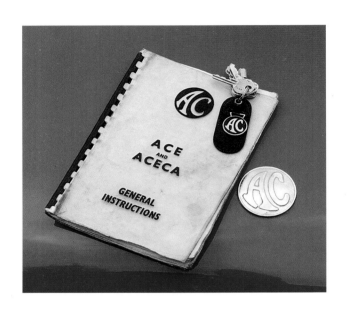